W9-CIK-318

What a Doll!

By Sara Corbett

Consultant: Susan Hedrick, Curator, Rosalie Whyel Museum of Doll Art

CHILDREN'S PRESS®
A Division of Grolier Publishing
New York   London   Hong Kong   Sydney
Danbury, Connecticut

Picture Acknowledgements

Cover (top left), NASA; cover (top right), © Jacksonville Museum of Contemporary Art, Collection of Walter P. Scott/ SuperStock; cover (bottom left), Copyright 1995 All Rights Reserved Rosalie Whyel Museum of Doll Art; cover (bottom right), © Chris Arend/Tony Stone Images; 1 (top), NASA; 1 (bottom), © Lani Novak Howe/Photri; 3 (top), © Lani Novak Howe/Photri; 3 (bottom right), © Lee Boltin; 3 (bottom left), Copyright 1995 All Rights Reserved Rosalie Whyel Museum of Doll Art; 4-5, © Chris Arend/Tony Stone Images; 4 (bottom left), © Cameramann International, Ltd.; 4 (top), Copyright 1995 All Rights Reserved Rosalie Whyel Museum of Doll Art; 5 (top), © Robert Frerck/Odyssey/Chicago; 5 (bottom), © Lani Novak Howe/Photri; 6 (left), © Daniel Aubry/Odyssey/Chicago; 6 (right), National Museum Belgrade/E.T. Archives, London/ SuperStock; 7 (top), British Museum, London/Bridgeman Art Library, London/SuperStock; 7 (bottom), Jacksonville Museum of Contemporary Art, Collection of Walter P. Scott/SuperStock; 8 (left), © E.W. Heirstead/Photri; 8-9, Corbis-Bettmann; 9 (right), © Lani Novak Howe/Photri; 9 (bottom), Copyright 1995 All Rights Reserved Rosalie Whyel Museum of Doll Art; 10 (left), © Robert Frerck/Odyssey/Chicago; 10 (center), Corbis-Bettmann; 10-11, © Wolfgang Kaehler; 11 (top), © Robert Frerck/ Odyssey/Chicago; 11 (bottom), © Dave G. Houser; 12 (left), © Betts Anderson/Unicorn Stock Photos; 12 (center), © Lani Novak Howe/Photri; 12-13, © Kurt Scholz/SuperStock; 13 (right), © Jean Higgins/Unicorn Stock Photos; 13 (bottom), © Lani Novak Howe/Photri; 14 (top left), Corbis-Bettmann; 14 (bottom), © Lani Novak Howe/Photri; 14-15, © Dave G. Houser; 15 (top right), © Geoff Tompkinson/Tony Stone Images; 15 (bottom), © Dave G. Houser; 16 (bottom), Copyright 1995 All Rights Reserved Rosalie Whyel Museum of Doll Art; 16 (top), Ackermann & Johnson Ltd./Bridgeman Art Library London/SuperStock; 17 (left), © Edward Cohen/SuperStock; 17 (right), Copyright 1995 All Rights Reserved Rosalie Whyel Museum of Doll Art; 18 (left and right), Copyright 1995 All Rights Reserved Rosalie Whyel Museum of Doll Art; 19 (top), Corbis-Bettmann; 19 (bottom left), © Frank Siteman/Photri; 19 (bottom right), AP/Wide World Photos; 20 (left), © Martin R..Jones/Unicorn Stock Photos; 20 (center), © Robert Frerck/Odyssey/Chicago; 20-21, © Tony Stone Images; 21 (right), © Michael Keith/SuperStock; 22 (left), © Victor Englebert; 22 (right), © Ray Manley/SuperStock; 23 (top left and bottom), © Victor Englebert; 23 (top right), © Cameramann International, Ltd.; 24 (left), © Lee Boltin; 24 (right), © SuperStock; 25 (top left), © John Elk III; 25 (top right), © Victor Englebert; 25 (bottom), © Myrleen Ferguson/PhotoEdit; 26 (left), © Dan McCoy/Rainbow; 26 (bottom right), © Mike Boroff/Photri; 26 (top right), © Lani Novak Howe; 27 (top), Copyright 1995 All Rights Reserved Rosalie Whyel Museum of Doll Art; 27 (bottom left), © Victor Englebert; 27 (right), © Frank Pennington/Unicorn Stock Photos; 28 (top), © Ann & Myron Sutton/SuperStock; 28 (bottom), Copyright 1995 All Rights Reserved Rosalie Whyel Museum of Doll Art; 29 (left), © Michael Rutherford/SuperStock; 29 (top right), AP/Wide World Photos; 29 (bottom), Corbis-Bettmann; 30 (left), Chip and Rosa Maria de la Cueva Peterson; 30 (right), Photri; 30-31, © Momatiuk/Eastcott/Valan; 31 (top right), Chip and Rosa Maria de la Cueva Peterson; 31 (bottom), © Jan Butchofsky.

On the cover

Top right: Ancient fertility figure, Mexico
c. 800 BC – AD 200
Bottom left: Chinese actor doll
Bottom right: Assortment of antique dolls,
Germany and France

On the title page

Handmade African doll

Project Editor Shari Joffe
Design Steve Marton
Photo Research Feldman & Associates

Corbett, Sara.
What a doll! / by Sara Corbett.
p. cm. — (A world of difference)
Includes index.
Summary: Discusses the history and appeal of dolls and how they play an important role in religion, work, celebration, and cultural tradition in many parts of the world.
ISBN 0-516-08211-6
1. Dolls — Juvenile literature. [1. Dolls.]
I. Title. II. Series.
NK 4893.C67 1996
745.592`21 — dc20

95-39664
CIP
AC

Contents

Miniature Marvels **4**

Early Dolls **6**

Wax, Clay, or Straw? **8**

Miniature Ambassadors **12**

All Dolled Up **16**

Famous Faces **18**

Celebrating with Dolls **20**

Believing in Dolls **22**

Practical Dolls **26**

Novelty Dolls **28**

A Doll's Best Friend **30**

Glossary **32**

Index **32**

Miniature Marvels

It's hard to dislike dolls. Why? Because they're miniature versions of who we are. If you look at a doll, you can often imagine a personality and sometimes even a story to fit the way it looks. Some dolls, for example, look delicate and young, like little princesses or princes. Other dolls look more like everyday people—they might be happy, thoughtful, or even stern. We imagine them to be like our parents, friends, or even our own pretend children! A doll's appearance will give you clues to its personality, but it's up to your imagination to fill in the rest.

An important clue is provided by the way a doll is dressed. A doll that wears a frilly silk dress, leather boots, a little straw hat and carries a parasol is probably not the kind of doll you'd have sleep next to you in bed! But a more simple doll, made of soft cloth and without fancy clothes, might make the perfect nighttime friend.

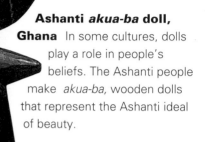

Ashanti *akua-ba* doll, Ghana In some cultures, dolls play a role in people's beliefs. The Ashanti people make *akua-ba*, wooden dolls that represent the Ashanti ideal of beauty.

***Matryoshka* dolls, Russia**
These wooden "nesting" dolls fit nicely inside of one another. Though nobody knows who was the first person to make them, the *Matryoshkas* are Russia's most famous dolls.

Puppets, India Puppets, found all over the world, are a type of doll used to tell a story.

Dolls are more than good companions, however. In many parts of the world, dolls play an important role in religion, work, celebration, and cultural tradition, too. In fact, if you take a good look, you may find that your dolls are more than toys, as well. Look at the dolls you see here and play detective for a minute: where do you think they come from? What kind of "personality" do they have? What might they be used for? Are their owners children or adults? Boys or girls?
See how much you can deduce!

Antique dolls, Germany and France Elegantly dressed dolls with heads made of bisque (unglazed porcelain) or wax were popular in Europe from the mid-1800s until the 1930s. More fragile than rag dolls, these dolls were usually intended for older children.

Raggedy Ann, United States In many cultures, a soft, easy-to-cuddle rag doll is a child's first toy. The Raggedy Ann doll was created by American illustrator Johnny Gruelle in 1918.

Early Dolls

Dolls have been around practically as long as humans. They have been found in the dwellings of prehistoric people as well as in the tombs of ancient Egyptian rulers. What we don't know about these very old dolls is exactly how they were used in these cultures. Archeologists—scientists whose job it is to put together all the clues to understand how ancient people

lived—believe that primitive dolls were actually not used as toys, but instead were taken very seriously. They believe that the miniature human figures made from clay and stone by people during the Stone Age (about 30,000 B.C.) were probably used in religious ceremonies. Dolls found in Egyptian tombs are thought to represent faithful servants who traveled with the dead ruler to the next world.

Stone-Age figure Figurines like this, made from stone, are hard to recognize as dolls, but it's believed they were carved to look like humans and then used in religious ceremonies by people more than 20,000 years ago.

Ancient Roman doll, c. 200 B.C. Wooden or clay doll-like figures with movable arms and legs have been found in Greek and Roman tombs. It is not known whether these dolls were playthings or religious objects.

Wooden "paddle" doll, Egypt, c. 500 B.C.
The tombs of the Egyptian pharaohs were often the size of small buildings and loaded with all sorts of treasures. Because rulers were often buried with small ceramic, glass, or wooden figures such as the one you see here, archeologists have theorized that the figures were meant to represent servants who would take care of the pharaoh as he moved from one world to the next.

Ancient fertility figure, Mexico, c. 800 B.C.–A.D. 200 Many ancient peoples made human figures out of clay or stone as *fetishes*—objects that are believed to contain powerful spirits. This fertility figure may have been used to help women bear children or help the community to have a good harvest.

There is evidence that the ancient Greek and Roman cultures had little cloth dolls that were actually used as toys. During the Middle Ages (476-1453 A.D.), a favorite form of entertainment was watching religious puppet shows put on by artists who traveled from village to village. (Remember, this was at least 500 years before television and movies were invented!) It's interesting to note that the word "puppet" comes from the Latin word *pupa,* which means—you guessed it!—"doll."

Wax, Clay, or Straw?

Have you ever owned a doll? If you have, where and how was it made? Today, most dolls are made in factories and then sold in stores. If you go to a toy store, you usually find a large selection of dolls. While it's fun to have a choice, there's something very special about dolls that don't come from factories— the kind of dolls that are handmade.

If you were going to make a doll today, what kind of materials would you use? Chances are, you won't be able to use the plastic or porcelain that's used in factories, so you'd have to be creative with the things in your own environment. You might find a good piece of wood, or some fun fabric to sew into a doll. What about a hunk of clay? A bottle? A sock?

Petites Constructions

imagerie d'Epinal. — PELLERIN, imp.-édit. (Déposé)

Paper doll with costumes, France, 1889 Paper dolls—whether handmade or store-bought—have long been a popular kind of doll because they're made from a material that is inexpensive and easily available.

Inupiat doll The Inupiat of Alaska have traditionally dressed their dolls in the furs of nearby arctic animals. This doll wears a ground-squirrel fur parka.

ETITES FILLES A HABILLER

No 50

Ne coller les coiffures que par le haut.

Sock monkey, United States
Handmade dolls are often made from household materials such as old socks or scraps of leftover fabric.

Spoon dolls, Bolivia These handcrafted dolls are made from something you might find in your own kitchen: wooden spoons! They are dressed in the brightly colored fabrics traditionally worn by people who live in the Andes mountains of Bolivia.

Ndebele doll, South Africa
The Ndebele people of South Africa are famous for their beaded jewelry, clothing, and dolls.

Painted wooden doll, Sweden
In northern European countries, where forests are plentiful, handcrafted dolls are often made of wood.

The truth is, with a little imagination, you can make a doll from just about anything. Throughout history, people have made creative use of the materials readily available in their own environments. For instance, when the pioneers settled in the Great Plains of the United States in the early 1800s, their lives revolved around growing corn, which flourished in the fertile soil of the Midwest. They slept on mattresses filled with corn husks, used strings of popcorn to decorate their Christmas trees, and even ate popcorn and milk for breakfast, the same way we eat cereal today! And, following the example of the Iroquois people, they even made dolls out of corn husks.

Plains Indian deerskin doll, 1800s On the North American plains, where deer and buffalo were plentiful, Indians traditionally made dolls from animal hide, beads, and hair.

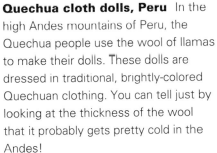

Quechua cloth dolls, Peru In the high Andes mountains of Peru, the Quechua people use the wool of llamas to make their dolls. These dolls are dressed in traditional, brightly-colored Quechuan clothing. You can tell just by looking at the thickness of the wool that it probably gets pretty cold in the Andes!

Straw doll, Bahamas The Bahamas are a group of islands in the Atlantic Ocean southeast of the United States. These dolls are made from straw, a material that is plentiful in the Bahamas.

Miniature Ambassadors

Because dolls are physical reflections of the humans who create them, they often reflect their maker's culture as well. A doll that's made in northern Russia, for instance, is not likely to look like one made in Mexico. Not only will each doll resemble the people of the region it comes from, but it will probably be dressed in the traditional clothing of that area, too.

Flower peddler doll, Portugal

Dolls in native costume, Estonia

Children in Swedish costume These days, it's less and less common to see people wearing the traditional dress of their region or country. For this reason, national folk dolls are more than souvenirs—they help record fashions and customs that are quickly disappearing.

Many dolls also give you a glimpse of the traditional life of its makers. Because dolls do such a good job representing culture, they are often sold as souvenirs or given as gifts for travelers to take back to their own countries.

Japanese doll This doll in traditional Japanese dress was a gift from Japan to the president of the United States.

***Gondolier* doll, Italy** The Italian city of Venice is an island that has canals instead of streets. This doll is dressed like a *gondolier*—a person who steers the long boats called *gondolas* down the canals.

Yarn dolls, Mexico Mexican dolls, often made of cloth or yarn, are usually outfitted in the lively colors of their region. These dolls are from Oaxaca, in southeastern Mexico.

Flamenco-dancer dolls, Spain

Handcrafted African doll

Puppet maker, Taiwan

Sami dolls, Finland These dolls show the traditional dress of the Sami people, who live in Lapland, a region in far-northern Europe. Can you guess anything about the climate in Lapland from the way the dolls are dressed?

All Dolled Up

Dolls come in every style, from the very simple to the very fancy. Simple dolls are usually the kind that don't break and can be carried or played with just about anywhere. Fancy dolls, however, are often made from more fragile materials, such as porcelain, wax, or clay, and this means they need some extra care so they don't break or fall apart.

In the United States and some European countries, owning a fancy doll was once thought to be a sign of one's wealth and position in society. Although these dolls were actually played with by children through the 1800s and early 1900s, today they are treated more like special treasures than like toys. Often, they are kept on shelves, in museums, or in dollhouses that are elegant enough to suit the fancy doll. Some people collect dolls as works of art!

19th-century painting of child with wax doll, England
Well-dressed, very fragile dolls like the one shown in this portrait were so precious that in some cases, children were only allowed to play with them on Sundays. The rest of the week, the dolls were put away on a shelf or in a drawer.

Parisian lady doll, c.1870
In France during the 1800s, dolls such as this were expensive toys for children of wealthy families. The child could obtain clothing, accessories, and furniture for the doll.

Warrior doll, Japan
This elaborately costumed Japanese doll depicts a *Samurai* warrior from the 1400s.

Manipuri dancer doll, India
Manipuri is one of the five classical dance styles of India. It originated in Manipur, a state in northeastern India, and usually portrays episodes in the life of Krishna, a Hindu god.

Even though the tradition of owning dolls just for show is one that belongs mostly to Western cultures, you can find dolls that represent the "perfect" person in cultures around the world.

Famous Faces

In many cultures, you'll find dolls modeled after famous people–entertainers, politicians, or members of royalty. Sometimes celebrity dolls mark a particular historic event, or celebrate a country's pride in its national identity. For example, when England crowns a new queen, as it did in 1837 with Queen Victoria, and again in 1952, with Queen Elizabeth II, dollmakers have fashioned dolls in the image of the new queen. Some of these dolls, first bought by loyal subjects to the queen, are very valuable collector's items.

Russian-leader Matryoshka dolls
Sometimes dolls comment on or poke fun at a country's politics or history. When the Soviet Union dissolved in 1990, these dolls began to appear in Russia. Borrowing the style of the traditional Matryoshka dolls, they humorously show a succession of prominent Russian leaders from Vladimir Lenin to Boris Yeltsin.

Chinese actor doll, 1930s
Because opera and theatre have been central to Chinese culture for many centuries, their stars are often very popular among the people of China. For this reason, artists often make delicate dolls to look like the current stars of the opera or theatre.

Michael Jackson doll, United States Dolls are often modeled after a culture's celebrities.

Marie-Therese of Austria, c. 1850 This doll, made in Germany in the 1800s, probably depicts the woman who became queen of France after she married King Louis XIV in 1660.

Queen Victoria doll, England, 1901 This doll was created to commemorate the death of Queen Victoria in 1901. She had reigned as queen of England for 64 years!

Celebrating with Dolls

Maybe because dolls are made to look like little humans, they actually have a lot to do with the way we relate to other people. In some cultures, dolls are regularly given as gifts. In other cultures, dolls are celebrated in their own festivals. In still others, dolls are used as part of a celebration, such as a marriage.

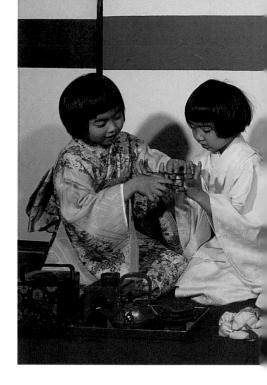

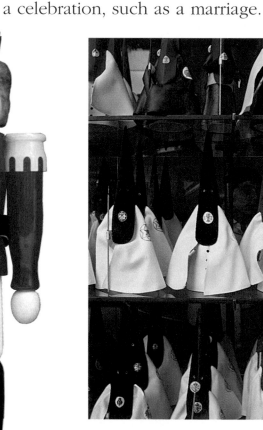

Nutcracker The nutcracker is a type of doll that has come to be associated with Christmas, thanks to a German folktale called "The Nutcracker and the Mouse King," which inspired the Christmas-story ballet *The Nutcracker*.

***Semana Santa* figures, Spain**
These dolls are sold during the celebration of *Semana Santa* (Holy Week), the week preceding Easter. The dolls represent members of special brotherhoods who walk in Holy Week processions dressed as penitents (people who ask God for forgiveness).

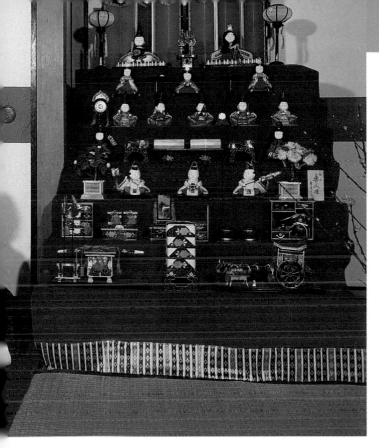

Day of the Dead doll, Mexico Skeleton figurines are a part of Day of the Dead, a happy celebration held in November all over Mexico to honor friends and relatives who have died. The skeleton dolls are meant to signify that the dead can actually be joyful and participate in the same things that living people do.

Girl's Doll Festival, Japan In Japan, boys and girls each have their own annual Doll Festival. On March 3 (for girls) and May 5 (for boys), each family brings out and displays special dolls that have been handed down for generations. Through the dolls, the children learn about their nation's history, as well as the qualities that are valued in men and women in Japanese culture. The girl's dolls include models of the Emperor and Empress and their court. The boys' dolls include *Samurai* warriors and legendary heroes.

In Syria, for example, it's a traditional custom for girls who are ready to be married to hang a small doll in their window to announce their availability. In India, beautifully dressed dolls were once given to child brides at their weddings.

Finally, because dolls can be just plain entertaining, they're often fun to have at a party!

Believing in Dolls

Not only are dolls involved in ritual celebrations, they are also a very important part of expressing beliefs. In fact, the history of dolls begins mostly with ceremonial or religious dolls, often called effigies, which were used to symbolize gods or people's offerings to the gods. Dolls are often used to represent a person, spirit, or god when that "person" can't be physically present.

Ancestor dolls, Indonesia Wooden dolls such as these are fairly common in Indonesia and much of the Eastern hemisphere. Carved to represent ancestors who have died, the dolls are kept in the family home and are thought to give the ancestors' spirits a happy resting place.

Hopi *kachina* figure The Hopi people of the southwestern United States have traditionally made *kachina* (spirit) figures, which are given to children so they can memorize the many gods of the Hopi tradition.

Ancestor figure, Benin As in Indonesian cultures, many African cultures make figures honoring dead ancestors because they believe it's important to provide ancestral spirits with a place to reside. Since African tradition honors elders as wise, these figures are often asked for advice or help in solving problems

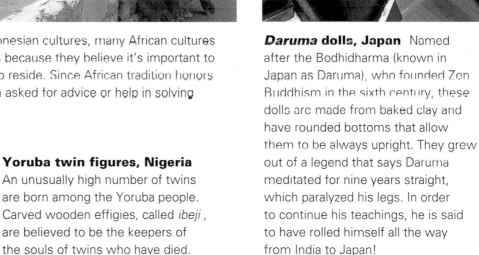

Daruma **dolls, Japan** Named after the Bodhidharma (known in Japan as Daruma), who founded Zen Buddhism in the sixth century, these dolls are made from baked clay and have rounded bottoms that allow them to be always upright. They grew out of a legend that says Daruma meditated for nine years straight, which paralyzed his legs. In order to continue his teachings, he is said to have rolled himself all the way from India to Japan!

Yoruba twin figures, Nigeria An unusually high number of twins are born among the Yoruba people. Carved wooden effigies, called *ibeji* , are believed to be the keepers of the souls of twins who have died.

The Yoruba people of Nigeria give birth to an unusual number of twins. Unfortunately, it is also fairly common for one of the twins to die while it is still an infant. When a twin dies, a wood figure called an *ibeji,* is carved to represent the dead twin. From then on, the wooden doll is dressed, fed, and taken care of just like its living twin.

Some dolls are thought to offer protection from evil spirits, or in some instances, to be the "scapegoat" and soak up any evil that might cause trouble for the humans it is guarding. Still others are used in ceremonies in which harm is wished on a certain person, who is represented by a doll. But even so, most dolls represent good spirits, and sometimes even good wishes, to bring happiness to the people that take care of them.

Inca grave-offering, ancient Peru This ancient cloth doll was originally used as a grave offering, to provide a deceased person with a companion so that he or she would not be lonely in the afterworld.

Shadow puppets, Java, Indonesia A very old Hindu tradition is to perform shadow plays with puppets made from animal hide, which, when held up before an oil lamp, cast long, lifelike shadows on the wall. The shadow play is thought to be a mirror of real life, showing that humans are just shadows moved by the hand of God.

Voodoo doll, Haiti Part of the practice of voodoo, a major religion on the island of Haiti, traditionally involves using dolls to represent the people you wish to suffer bad fortune or illness. Practicers of voodoo would stick a doll with needles or burn it, believing a similar ill fate would befall the person it's meant to represent.

Ashanti girl with *akua-ba* doll, Ghana The Ashanti people make *akua-ba*, wooden dolls that represent the Ashanti ideal of beauty. Young girls and pregnant women carry these dolls in their wastebands so that they will have beautiful babies.

Crèche dolls, United States Made from anything from clay to wood to marble, the crèche, showing the birth scene of Jesus Christ, is a central part of the Christian tradition. All over the world, Christians display crèches at Christmastime.

Practical Dolls

So maybe dolls are fun toys and good representations of culture. They may be good symbols for religious beliefs and values. But are there dolls that are simply useful? Yes, actually!

Tea-cozy doll, Russia This doll doubles as a "tea-cozy" —its skirt fits over a pot of tea and keeps it warm!

Medicine doll, Japan This doll is used to teach the ancient healing art of acupuncture. It shows 660 spots on the body believed to be pressure points.

Baby doll Baby dolls are more than comforting friends— they can help children learn about caring for others.

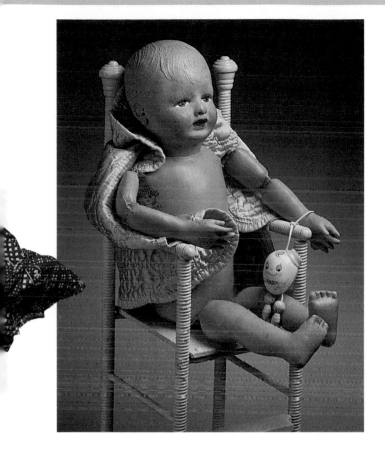

Chase hospital doll Invented by a woman named Martha Chase in 1910, this doll was used in hospitals to train student nurses in handling babies, feeding them, and giving them certain treatments.

Scarecrow, United States Farmers put up scarecrows to frighten away birds and animals that might eat their crops.

Store mannequins, Paraguay These may look more like real people than dolls, but mannequins sell clothes in a way that salespeople can't.

Novelty Dolls

A novelty is something that's unusual and just the opposite of practical—something just for fun! As technology has advanced, many enterprising inventors have set their minds to figuring out how to make dolls more realistic. While at one time, dolls were simply figures that looked like humans, since the 1800s there have been dolls that talk, walk, cry, and eat. Other dolls are not realistic, but they have special features that make them unusual or novel.

Pull-string doll, Germany This wooden doll has arms and legs that move with the tug of a string. In France during the 1700s, a similar doll, called a *pantin,* was often brought out at parties to do a crazy dance for the amusement of guests.

Ondine, the swimming doll, France, c. 1900
Created by a French inventor in 1876, "Ondine" has a body made of cork, and arms and legs that move as if making swimming strokes.

Ventriloquist and dummy Ventriloquists are entertainers who can "throw" their voices so it sounds as if they're carrying on a conversation with a "dummy" or puppet. One of the most famous ventriloquist-dummy teams of all time was Edgar Bergen and his wooden friend Charlie McCarthy.

Walking circus doll, England, early 1900s By winding a key, you can get this doll to skate across the room. Mechanical walking dolls have been around since the 1700s.

Mr. Potato Head, United States This plastic doll, a favorite of American children, comes equipped with several different kinds of removable eyes, ears, noses, mouths, hats, and shoes.

A Doll's Best Friend

Now that you've seen how interesting, fun, and educational dolls can be, it's important to remember that when it comes right down to it, dolls will always make great friends. The bigger your imagination is, the more fun you can have with dolls. No matter how simple, how fancy, how realistic, or how unusual your doll is, it takes only a little creativity for you to see that you've got a friend to talk to, play with, and take care of. Although the world is a large place, and people and cultures can be very different from one another, one thing that we all share is a love of playing. And what better playmate to have than a loyal, trustworthy doll?

Action-hero dolls, Japan

Kids with Cabbage Patch dolls, Canada

Ecuador

Inuit girl and
friend

Mexico

Glossary

acupuncture a Chinese practice of piercing the body with needles at specific points to cure disease or relieve pain (p. 26)

ancestors relatives who lived in the past (p. 23)

ancient very old (p. 7)

antique something made long ago (p. 5)

ceramic made of clay (p. 7)

commemorate to honor or keep fresh the memory of (p. 19)

companion a person who goes with another person; friend (p. 5)

culture the beliefs and customs of a group of people that are passed down from one generation to another (p. 4)

deceased dead (p. 24)

environment a person's natural surroundings (p. 10)

fashioned created (p. 18)

flourish to grow well; thrive (p. 10)

fragile easily broken or damaged (p. 5)

ideal perfect (p. 4)

mannequin a life-sized human dummy used to display clothing in a store (p. 27)

meditate to spend time in quiet thinking (p. 23)

miniature very small (p. 4)

participate to take part in (p. 21)

pharaoh a ruler of ancient Egypt (p. 7)

porcelain a fine hard pottery that was first produced in China (p. 8)

precious valuable (p. 16)

prehistoric occurring before the time when humans began recording history through writing (p. 6)

primitive coming from or belonging to the earliest times (p. 6)

procession a group of people or vehicles arranged one behind the other and moving in a formal way; parade (p. 20)

resemble to look like (p. 11)

scapegoat a person or group made to bear the blame for the sins or errors of others (p. 24)

souvenir an object that is kept as a reminder of the past (p. 11)

symbol something that stands for or represents something else (p. 26)

technology the scientific methods and ideas used in industry and trade (p. 28)

tradition a custom that is handed down from generation to generation (p. 5)

Index

Africa, 14
ancestor dolls, 22, 23
archeologists, 6
baby dolls, 26
Bahamas, 11
beliefs, 22-25
Benin, 23
Bolivia, 9
Canada, 30
celebrations, 21-22
Chase hospital doll, 27
China, 18
clay, 6, 8, 22
cloth, 7, 8, 11, 24
clothes for dolls, 4, 8, 9, 11, 12, 13, 15, 16, 17
corn husks, 10
crèche dolls, 25
culture and dolls, 12-13
deerskin, 11
doll festivals, 21
early dolls, 6-7
Ecuador, 30
Egypt, 6, 7
England, 5, 19
Estonia, 12
famous people, 18-19
fancy dolls, 16-17
fetishes, 7
Finland, 15
France, 8, 28
Germany, 18, 20, 28
Ghana, 4, 25
grave offerings, 24
Greeks, 7
Haiti, 25
Hopi people, 22

India, 5, 17, 21
Indonesia, 22, 24
Inuit people, 31
Inupiat people, 8
Italy, 13
Japan, 13, 17, 21, 22, 26, 30
kachina dolls, 22
mannequins, store, 27
Matryoshka dolls, 4, 19
Mexico, 7, 12, 14, 21, 31
Ndebele people, 10
Nigeria, 22
novelty dolls, 28-29
nutcrackers, 20
paper dolls, 8
Paraguay, 27
Peru, 11, 24
Plains Indians, 11
Portugal, 12
puppets, 5, 7, 14, 24
religion, 5, 6, 7
Romans, 6, 7
Russia, 5, 12, 26
scarecrows, 27
Spain, 14, 20
spoon dolls, 9
Sweden, 10, 12
Syria, 21
Taiwan, 15
United States, 5, 9, 16, 19, 22, 25, 27, 29
voodoo dolls, 25
wax, 16
wood, 6, 7, 8, 10, 22, 23, 25, 28
yarn, 14
Yoruba people, 23

About the Author

Sara Corbett is a writer who lives in Santa Fe, New Mexico. This book is dedicated to her grandmother, who once travelled throughout Europe and brought a doll from nearly every country she visited home to her granddaughter.